The Official Character Guide

DIGITAL
DIGIMON
MONSTERS
™

A. Ryan Nerz

HarperEntertainment
An Imprint of HarperCollinsPublishers

HarperEntertainment
An Imprint of HarperCollins*Publishers*
10 East 53rd Street, New York, NY 10022–5299

ISBN 0-06-107184-6

Book design and composition by Diane Hobbing of Snap-Haus Graphics

Book production by Bill Schiffmiller & Keith Conover

All art © 2000 by Toei Animation

First printing: June 2000

Printed in the United States of America

Visit HarperEntertainment on the World Wide Web at www.harpercollins.com

10 9 8 7 6 5 4 3 2 1

WELCOME TO THE DIGITAL WORLD!

Just imagine it: I'm soaking up the sun during some free time at summer camp. Suddenly, the clouds turn black, and it starts snowing like crazy . . . in August! I was freaked out! And that was just the beginning. A strange sensation came over me. I can't explain it. It was like I dissolved in water, turned into nothing for a split second, and then . . . poof! I was whisked away with six of my camp friends to this weird island filled with hundreds of . . . monsters!

I know. You probably think I'm crazy. I have a hard time believing it myself.

I haven't seen my parents in days. The only humans I ever see are my six buddies. But I'll introduce you to them in a minute. I have to tell you about the Digimon first!

So I'm sitting there on this island, right, and out of nowhere comes a bouncing ball of a creature with floppy ears and sharp teeth. I swear! And the little ball speaks to me. The little guy—I mean, I guess it's a guy—says his name is "Koromon."

3

Koromon said he was a Digimon, a Digital Monster, and that he had come to be my guide and protector in the Digital World. He said there were hundreds more like him, and some of them were enormous and vicious beast-monsters. What was I supposed to say? Besides, the little guy was kind of cute, and I was totally lost.

The DigiWorld

"What exactly is a *Digi*World?" I asked him.

Koromon explained. "It stands for Digital World. It's a world where everything, even me, is made of digital material."

Digital material? Just the thought made my brain hurt, but I thought I was starting to get the picture.

"So how much do you weigh, Koromon?" I asked. "Nothing?"

Koromon looked at me and smiled. "You're a smart one," he said. "I am not measured in pounds like you, but in terms of memory, or Gigabytes. I weigh 10.0 Gigabytes."

Wow. This was getting stranger by the second. "So is everything around me— the trees and the sky and everything— digital?" I asked.

"Sure is," Koromon said. "Check it out for yourself."

I climbed up a tree to have a look at this Digital World.

There were beautiful forests and mountains and water in the distance, kind of like, well, California. But something was different. It was as if the whole world was being displayed on a computer screen. Does that make sense? Do you still think I'm crazy?

Well, you'll definitely think I'm crazy when I get to this next part. I was checking out this computerized world with my binoculars . . . when I spotted an enormous red beetle with huge pinchers and claws flying right toward me and shrieking!

I later found out that he was another Digimon named Kuwagamon, who's notorious for his dangerous Scissor Claw attack technique. Luckily, my little ball of a friend, Koromon, was a lot braver than he looked.

Then again, it's probably easier to be brave when you can change, or "digivolve" into a bigger, tougher creature. Wait a second. I haven't explained that part yet.

Digivolution

So there's Koromon, trying to defend me against this humongous red beast. And he was brave for a little guy. But his only power to defend me against Kuwagamon was an attack called the Bubble Blow. It's about as effective as it sounds.

So Kuwagamon was shrieking wildly, fending off bubbles, and basically, about to eat me and my friends for breakfast. All of a sudden, Koromon was swept up in a little mini-tornado and—whoosh!—Koromon vanished before my eyes. And in his place appeared an orange dinosaur-like creature with long arms and claws. His name was Agumon.

Well, Agumon started shooting these fireballs out of his mouth at Kuwagamon, a technique called Pepper Breath. It was the coolest thing I've ever seen! I mean, Agumon didn't exactly win the battle, but he saved me from getting chomped on by Kuwagamon.

And then, after the battle ended, Agumon changed back into Koromon. Right before my eyes! Are you confused? So was I.

Koromon explained it all to me. He said that his job was to defend me in the DigiWorld. But he wasn't powerful enough to defend me against huge, powerful Digimons like Kuwagamon. So he combined his power with my digivices to digivolve into a more powerful creature. Digivices are these little devices that look like beepers.

ROOKIE

I don't know where mine came from. It just appeared on my belt when I landed in the Digital World. But it works! When

Koromon's power and my digivices combine, he can grow (or digivolve) to the next level . . . and beyond!

You see, every Digimon has a certain level or ranking, and Koromon's level is In-Training. When he focuses on growing, though, Koromon digivolves into his Rookie state, called Agumon.

CHAMPION

ULTIMATE

It gets better. Koromon can get even stronger and change into his Champion state, Greymon, a gigantic orange one-horned beast that really kicks butt.

And then, if Koromon gets really revved up, he can turn into his Ultimate form, Metal-Greymon. MetalGreymon is so intimidating that he even scares me.

You'd think that, with MetalGreymon on my side, no Digimons in the DigiWorld would scare me in the slight-est. But you'd be surprised. There are some Digimons, especially the evil ones, that even MetalGreymon can't defeat.

Evil Digimons & Black Gears

We've made a pretty important discovery about some of the evil Digimons around here. It's this: They're not all actually evil. In fact, they're usually good. They've just got something bad stuck inside them. Let me explain.

The first time we found out about the Black Gears was when Meramon attacked us.

Meramon is this huge flaming creature who guards Mount Miharashi. He's a Champion Digimon, and he's supposed to be a really nice dude. *Supposed* to be.

Our Digimons told us not to worry about Meramon at all. Boy, were they wrong! First of all, he used his fireballs to dry up the lake right next to our friends the Pyokomons' village. Then, out of nowhere, Meramon attacked us! It was one of the scariest things that's ever happened to me. Imagine a huge flaming beast hurling fireballs at you!

Well, luckily, Biyomon, Sora's Digimon, digivolved into Birdramon and saved the day. When Birdramon defeated Meramon, the weirdest thing happened. This Black Gear came flying through the air and shattered right near us.

And just like that, Meramon was a nice guy again. He even sat down on the ground and talked to us! He said that he didn't know why he had attacked us, that it was out of his control. It was the Black Gear that made him do it. And those Black Gears are everywhere. They're causing a lot of problems in the DigiWorld, turning a lot of good Digimons into bad ones. The only question is: *Why?*

We don't know. Maybe you can help us figure it out.

My Friends & Their Digimons

Am I forgetting something? Oh yeah! I forgot to tell you about all my friends and their Digimons. Oops! Well, first of all, let me tell you one interesting thing: the companion Digimons seem to fit our personalities. Mimi shoots the breeze with Tanemon about her hair. My Digimon is tough like me. And, well . . . let me just introduce them all to you.

How to Use the Digimon Guide

Pronunciation: **This is how to say the Digimon's name.**

Number: **Every Digimon has a number! If you're not sure what number a particular Digimon has, there is an alphabetical index in the back of this book.**

Game Card Number: **Many Digimons are included in the Digi-Battle Card Game. This number corresponds to their card in the game.**

Trading Card Number: **Some Digimons have their very own trading cards. This number corresponds to their trading card if they have one.**

Digimon Level: **Each Digimon is assigned a level of digivolution. The five different levels are as follows, in order of least advanced to most advanced: In-Training, Rookie, Champion, Ultimate, and Mega.**

Digimon Group: **There are several different groups of Digimons, including Micro Digimons, Sea Animal Digimons, Evil Digimons, and so on. Often, these groups relate to the type of animal or creature that the Digimon resembles. For example, Greymon looks like a dinosaur, so his group is Dinosaur Digimon.**

**Digimon Type: Digimons are made of
three different types of digital material:
Data, Virus, and Vaccine. Not every Digimon
has a type.**

**Data Size (G): This measures the size of each
Digimon, in Gigabytes. It is roughly the same as
the Digamon's actual physical size. For example, the
smaller In-Training Digimons range from 4.0 to 10.0 G in size.
Champion Digimons are larger, ranging from 10.0 G to 40.0 G.**

**Technique: Each Digimon has two attack techniques. The
first technique is usually the first they try. For example,
"Bubble Blow." The second attack technique is
often used if the first was unsuccessful. For
example, "Thunder Javelin."**

**Special Ability: There are only three types of
special abilities: Flying, Swimming, and
Digging. Approximately half of the Digimons
possess one of these abilities.**

**Description: What are the Digimon's special
characteristics? What does it look like?
Read the Description to find out.**

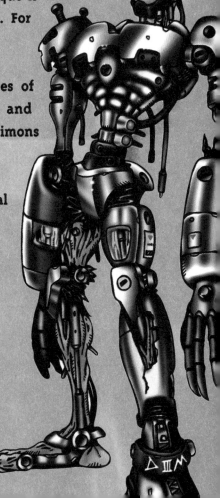

"TAI" TAICHI HAMIYA

I guess I should tell you a little about myself. Hmm. Well, back home I was the athletic type—I played every sport I could, from baseball to badminton. But I haven't found any baseball leagues here in DigiWorld, and now I only use my athletic ability to keep us from getting squashed by giant Digimons. Some say I'm a natural leader, but it's probably just because I'm hyper. I can't sit still for a second. I heard one of my friends say that I have "the attention span of a gnat," which is true. When I get bored, I'm usually just eager for the next adventure. Sometimes I take off on my own, and the others follow me. And I have to admit it: more than once, I've led the gang right smack into the middle of trouble.

Koromon

Pronunciation: **KOR-OH-MON**

Number: **1**

Trading Card Number: **4**

Digimon Level: **In-Training**

Digimon Group: **Micro**

Data Size (G): **10.0**

Technique: **Bubble Blow**

Second Technique: **None**

Special Ability: **None**

Description: **Koromon's name means "brave little monster," and that's exactly what he is. Actually, he's more like a bouncing ball of digi-energy. His data size is only 10.0 G, but don't let the size fool you. I thought Koromon would be a total wimp when I first met him. But he's not. Even though his only attack is the Bubble Blow, Koromon doesn't back down from Champion Digimons like Kuwagamon!**

Koromon digivolves into . . .

Agumon

Pronunciation: **AH-GOO-MON**

Number: **8**

Game Card Number: **St-01**

Trading Card Number: **11**

Digimon Level: **Rookie**

Digimon Group: **Reptile**

Digimon Type: **Vaccine**

Data Size (G): **20.0**

Technique: **Pepper Breath**

Second Technique: **Claw Attack**

Special Ability: **None**

ROOKIE

Description: **Agumon is like an orange, overgrown lizard with an extra dose of pep. In fact, he came up with a fight song for the crew: "Digimon eat! Digimon fight! Digimon, Digimon fight all night!" Agumon also has Pepper Breath, which is so strong that it starts fires on impact. When that doesn't work, this Rookie Digimon uses his pointy claws for a vicious Claw Attack. Agumon is humble by nature, but Tai has told him he's "the man" so often that he might start to believe it.**

Agumon digivolves into . . .

Greymon

CHAMPION

Pronunciation: **GRAY-MON**
Number: **16**
Game Card Number: **St-02**
Trading Card Number: **18**
Digimon Level: **Champion**
Digimon Group: **Dinosaur**

Digimon Type: **Vaccine**
Data Size (G): **30.0**
Technique: **Nova Blast**
Second Technique: **Great Horns Attack**
Special Ability: **None**
Description: **Greymon (whose name means "gray monster") is a much bigger, scarier version of Agumon. He looks like an orange *Tyrannosaurus rex* with a rhinoceros mask on. When Greymon attacks, he spits forth a Nova Blast that looks like a stream of speeding fireballs. If it weren't for the Nova Blast that Greymon used to destroy the evil Shellmon, we wouldn't have made it past our first day in the DigiWorld!**

Greymon digivolves into . . .

MetalGreymon

Pronunciation: **MEH-TUL-GRAY-MON**

Number: **54**

Game Card Number: **B0-01**

Trading Card Number: **39**

Digimon Level: **Ultimate**

Digimon Group: **Android**

Digimon Type: **Vaccine**

Data Size (G): **40.0**

Technique: **Giga Blaster**

Second Technique: **Mega Claw**

Special Ability: **Flying**

Description: **If a mad scientist made a vicious dinosaur out of steel, it might look like MetalGreymon. Long claws, gnashing teeth, and a giant hook of a tail—all made of metal. And MetalGreymon's attack techniques make him even more intimidating. Only other monstrous Ultimate Digimons can fend off his Giga Blaster, and his Mega Claw is equally feared.**

MetalGreymon digivolves into . . .

WarGreymon

MEGA

Pronunciation: **WORE-GRAY-MON**

Number: **90**

Digimon Level: **Mega**

Digimon Group: **Dinosaur**

Digimon Type: **Vaccine**

Data Size (G): **20.0**

Technique: **Nova Force**

Second Technique: **Mega Claw**

Special Ability: **Flying**

Description: *Tyrannosaurus rex* on steroids. That's the best way to describe this Dinosaur Digimon. Whew! Is this dude scary or what? He has a strange ability to collect energy from all over the place and concentrate it in the palm of his hand. Then he can shoot it back out again at anyone who dares try to attack him.

DIGIVOLVE

"MATT" YAMATO ISHIDA

Matt thinks he's the coolest guy on the planet. (That is, if we're still on the planet.) When I introduce him to someone, Matt's the type to say, "No autographs, please." But I don't think he really means it—he's just acting. And, between you and me, Matt actually is pretty cool. I think it's cool that, even though he won't admit it, Matt is really protective of his little brother, T.K. It annoys me sometimes when Matt doesn't listen to my directions. But he does tell funny jokes, and sometimes at night, he plays a mean harmonica. If we ever get out of the DigiWorld, I wouldn't be surprised if Matt became a rock star or something.

Tsunomon

IN-TRAINING

Pronunciation: **SOO-NOH-MON**

Number: **2**

Trading Card Number: **6**

Digimon Level: **In-Training**

Digimon Group: **Micro**

Data Size (G): **10.0**

Technique: **Bubble Blow**

Special Ability: **None**

Description: **Tsunomon's** like Matt: cool. I mean, it might seem weird to call a little orange fuzzy monster with a dolphin's fin on top of his head *cool*, but he is. Tsunomon is always calm under pressure. And even though he has only the Bubble Blow to defend himself, he'll stand up and fight against the toughest Digimon in DigiWorld.

Tsunomon digivolves into . . .

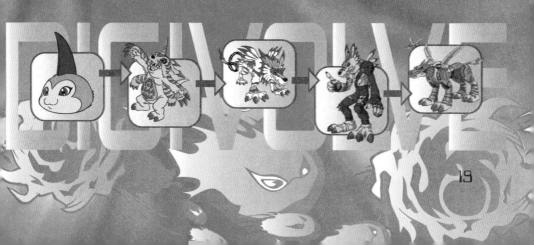

Gabumon

Pronunciation: **GAH-BOO-MON**

Number: **9**

Game Card Number: **St-05**

Trading Card Number: **13**

Digimon Level: **Rookie**

Digimon Group: **Reptile**

Digimon Type: **Data**

Data Size (G): **20.0**

Technique: **Blue Blaster**

Second Technique: **Horn Attack**

Special Ability: **None**

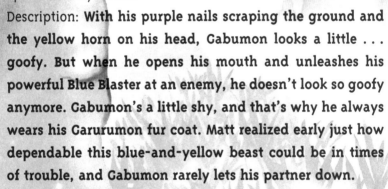

Description: **With his purple nails scraping the ground and the yellow horn on his head, Gabumon looks a little . . . goofy. But when he opens his mouth and unleashes his powerful Blue Blaster at an enemy, he doesn't look so goofy anymore. Gabumon's a little shy, and that's why he always wears his Garurumon fur coat. Matt realized early just how dependable this blue-and-yellow beast could be in times of trouble, and Gabumon rarely lets his partner down.**

Gabumon digivolves into . . .

Garurumon

Pronunciation: **GAH-ROO-ROO-MON**

Number: **18**

Game Card Number: **St–06**

Trading Card Number: **20**

Digimon Level: **Champion**

Digimon Group: **Animal**

CHAMPION

Digimon Type: **Vaccine**

Data Size (G): **20.0**

Technique: **Howling Blaster**

Second Technique: **Slamming Attack**

Special Ability: **None**

Description: **Garurumon** looks like a great snow wolf. And he howls like one, too! His Howling Blaster blows the enemy away like a sonic gun. Seadramon learned the hard way when Garurumon almost howled him into the bottom of the ocean.

Garurumon digivolves into . . .

WereGarurumon

Pronunciation: **WAIR-GAH-ROO-ROO-MON**

Number: **56**

Game Card Number: **St-47**

Trading Card Number: **U7**

Digimon Level: **Ultimate**

Digimon Group: **Animal**

Digimon Type: **Vaccine**

Data Size (G): **18.0**

Technique: **Mega Claw**

Second Technique: **Garuru Kick**

Special Ability: **None**

Description: **If you think Garurumon is scary, you haven't seen WereGarurumon . . . because he looks like Garurumon at a punk-rock concert! With spikes on his knees and knuckles, WereGarurumon doesn't have to use his Mega Claw attack to defend Matt. He just has to show up!**

WereGarurumon digivolves into . . .

MetalGarurumon

Pronunciation: **MEH-TUL-GAH-ROO-ROO-MON**

Number: **91**

Digimon Level: **Mega**

Digimon Group: **Android**

Digimon Type: **Vaccine**

Data Size (G): **28.0**

Technique: **Metal Wolf Claw**

Second Technique: **Metal Slamming Attack**

Special Ability: **None**

Description: **This Digimon is really cold. When he wants to** defeat the enemy he just breathes out his super chilly breath and freezes his opponents until they turn to ice—and shatter like ice. Definitely wear a scarf around this guy.

23

Sora's kind of like the older sister I never had. She lets me think that I'm leading the gang, but I can tell she's always keeping an eye on me. Sora's first concern is for everyone's safety. But she's a total tomboy, and I can tell that she actually wants to throw herself headfirst into the next adventure. But because she's worried about our safety, Sora usually holds herself back and watches over the rest of us (which is a good thing).

24

Yokomon

Pronunciation: **YOH-KOH-MON**

Number: **3**

Trading Card Number: **5**

Digimon Level: **In-Training**

Digimon Group: **Micro**

Data Size (G): **4.0**

Technique: **Bubble Blow**

Special Ability: **Flying**

Description: **Yokomon is probably the cutest Digimon I've ever seen. She looks like a little pink** flower with shiny green eyes and a blue blossom on top of her head. I hate to say it, but toughness is not Yokomon's strong point. (Then again, she is the smallest Digimon in DigiWorld.) She also has been know to fly for short distances, which can really come in handy in a pinch. Just like Sora, Yokomon is the voice of reason, and she never loses faith that the good guys will come out on top.

IN-TRAINING

Yokomon digivolves into . . .

Biyomon

Pronunciation: **BEE-YOH-MON**

Number: **10**

Game Card Number: **St-03**

Trading Card Number: **12**

Digimon Level: **Rookie**

Digimon Group: **Bird**

Digimon Type: **Vaccine**

Data Size (G): **15.0**

Technique: **Spiral Twister**

Second Technique: **Pecking Attack**

Special Ability: **None**

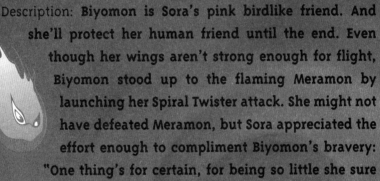

ROOKIE

Description: **Biyomon** is Sora's pink birdlike friend. And she'll protect her human friend until the end. Even though her wings aren't strong enough for flight, Biyomon stood up to the flaming Meramon by launching her Spiral Twister attack. She might not have defeated Meramon, but Sora appreciated the effort enough to compliment Biyomon's bravery: "One thing's for certain, for being so little she sure has a huge heart."

Biyomon digivolves into . . .

Birdramon

CHAMPION

Pronunciation: **BURD-RAH-MON**

Number: **21**

Game Card Number: **St-04**

Trading Card Number: **19**

Digimon Level: **Champion**

Digimon Group: **Bird**

Digimon Type: **Vaccine**

Data Size (G): **30.0**

Technique: **Meteor Wing**

Second Technique: **Fire Flapping**

Special Ability: **Flying**

Description: **Biyomon may not have been able to defeat Meramon, but then she digivolved into . . . Birdramon! And Birdramon, who looks like a hawk from the days of dinosaurs, came swooping down from the sky to blitz Meramon with his Meteor Wing! Birdramon's firepower was so effective that he didn't even have to utilize his Fire Flapping technique.**

Birdramon digivolves into . . .

Garudamon

Pronunciation: **GAH-ROO-DAH-MON**

Number: **65**

Game Card Number: **Bo—89**

Trading Card Number:

Digimon Level: **Ultimate**

Digimon Group: **Bird**

Digimon Type: **Vaccine**

Data Size (G): **25.0**

Technique: **Wing Blade**

Second Technique: **None**

Special Ability: **None**

Description: **Just when you thought a bird could get no tougher than Birdramon . . . he digivolves into Garudamon! Garudamon looks like a strange combination between an enormous person and an even bigger bird. Garudamon's Wing Blade technique is so destructive that he doesn't even need a second technique to back it up.**

"IZZY" HOUSHIRO IZUMI

Izzy might be the smartest kid I know. And there's really only one way to describe him—Izzy's a computer nerd. One of the first questions I heard him ask about DigiWorld was: "Do you have Internet access?" He carries his laptop computer with him everywhere he goes. CDs make him think about information storage, not about his favorite rock band. But I have to give the little runt a hand—he's pretty brave, and his understanding of computers sure has come in handy in this digital world.

Motimon

IN-TRAINING

Pronunciation: **MOH-TEE-MON**

Number: **4**

Game Card Number:

Trading Card Number: **7**

Digimon Level: **In-Training**

Digimon Group: **Micro**

Data Size (G): **8.0**

Technique: **Bubble Blow**

Second Technique: **None**

Special Ability: **None**

Description: **Motimon** is just like Izzy—small and spunky, but he has the tendency to bulge up when he's excited. He looks like a cute little ghost with black eyes and a constant smile. And Motimon's really smart, too—he helps Izzy see that true genius is not just understanding computers, but using them creatively to help others.

Motimon digivolves into . . .

Tentomon

Pronunciation: **TENT-OH-MON**

Number: **11**

Game Card Number: **St–07**

Trading Card Number: **14**

Digimon Level: **Rookie**

Digimon Group: **Insectoid**

Digimon Type: **Vaccine**

Data Size (G): **15.0**

Technique: **Super Shocker**

Second Technique: **Talon Attack**

Special Ability: **Flying**

Description: **Tentomon buzzes around like a huge red mosquito. Unlike a mosquito, though, Tentomon has enormous claws, a hard shell that protects him from danger, and a lethal attack technique called the Super Shocker! He takes aim at the opponent's weak spot and unleashes a lightning rod of electricity. For all his fierce powers, Tentomon is really gentle deep down. But with his shocking power and his sharp talons, Tentomon has trouble defending Izzy only when he's up against Champion Digimons.**

Tentomon digivolves into . . .

ROOKIE

Kabuterimon

Pronunciation: **KAB-OOH-TEER-EE-MON**

Number: **23**

Game Card Number: **St—08**

Trading Card Number: **21**

Digimon Level: **Champion**

Digimon Group: **Insectoid**

Digimon Type: **Vaccine**

Data Size (G): **30.0**

Technique: **Electro Shocker**

Second Technique: **Beetle Horn Attack**

Special Ability: **Flying**

Description: **As scary as Kabuterimon looks, he's a good Digimon. Thank goodness. Because Kabuterimon's four clawed arms, three sets of teeth, razor-sharp horn, and flying power make him a pretty difficult Digimon to defeat in battle. Just ask the mighty Centarumon, who was zapped with Kabuterimon's Electro Shocker during a battle at the Dino ruins.**

Kabuterimon digivolves into . . .

MegaKabuterimon

Pronunciation: **MEH-GAH-KAH-BOO-TEER-EE-MON**

Number: **87**

Game Card Number: **St—28/98**

Trading Card Number: **41**

Digimon Level: **Ultimate**

Digimon Group: **Insectoid**

Digimon Type: **Vaccine**

Data Size (G): **30.0**

Technique: **Horn Buster**

Second Technique: **Electro Shocker**

Special Ability: **Flying**

Description: **Take the monster in your worst nightmare. Then multiply it by ten, and color it maroon. That's MegaKabuterimon. He uses the horns on his head to annihilate opponents with his lethal Horn Buster attack. It is so vicious that he rarely has to resort to the Electro Shocker attack.**

MIMI TACHIKAWA

Mimi's such a girly *girl*. Right after she met her Digimon, Tanemon, Mimi asked her new friend who had done her hair. Can you believe that? She's the type that doesn't like huge, dangerous monsters because she thinks they're too icky. But even though she acts a little ditzy, Mimi really knows what's going on. And I guess she doesn't look so bad in that cowboy hat she always wears.

Tanemon

IN-TRAINING

Pronunciation: **TAH-NEE-MON**

Number: **5**

Game Card Number:

Trading Card Number: **9**

Digimon Level: **In-Training**

Digimon Group: **Micro**

Data Size (G): **10.0**

Technique: **Bubble Blow**

Second Technique: **Digging**

Special Ability: **None**

Description: **Tanemon is pretty and girly, just like Mimi. Her name means "seed monster," and the green leaves sprouting from her head make Tanemon look like a living plant, but she's much more than that. Tanemon jumps into the most dangerous situations with reckless abandon, but she can also burrow underground to hide from danger. After the battle is over, Tanemon gossips with Mimi about hairdos and other girly stuff.**

Tanemon digivolves into . . .

Palmon

Pronunciation: **PAL-MON**

Number: **12**

Game Card Number: **St—09**

Trading Card Number: **16**

Digimon Level: **Rookie**

Digimon Group: **Vegetation**

Digimon Type: **Data**

Data Size (G): **15.0**

Technique: **Poison Ivy**

Second Technique: **Stinking Attack**

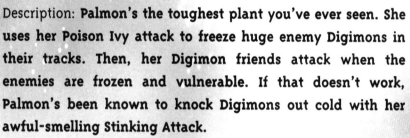

Description: **Palmon's the toughest plant you've ever seen. She uses her Poison Ivy attack to freeze huge enemy Digimons in their tracks. Then, her Digimon friends attack when the enemies are frozen and vulnerable. If that doesn't work, Palmon's been known to knock Digimons out cold with her awful-smelling Stinking Attack.**

Palmon digivolves into . . .

Togemon

CHAMPION

Pronunciation: **TOH-GEE-MON**

Number: **25**

Game Card Number: **St—10**

Trading Card Number: **26**

Digimon Level: **Champion**

Digimon Group: **Vegetation**

Digimon Type: **Data**

Data Size (G): **20.0**

Technique: **Needle Spray**

Second Technique: **Light Speed Jabbing**

Special Ability: **None**

Description: **Imagine running into an enormous cactus plant with legs, arms . . . and boxing gloves! Now imagine that the creature starts spraying its needles at you. Well, that's what it would be like to face Togemon, the toughest cactus in DigiWorld (or anywhere else, for that matter). And if the Needle Spray weren't enough, Togemon can attack with a lightning-quick power punch, like he did when he pummeled Cockatrimon. If you ever pick a fight with a plant, make sure it's not Togemon!**

Togemon digivolves into . . .

Lillymon

ULTIMATE

Pronunciation: **LIH-LEE-MON**

Number: **78**

Game Card Number: **Bo-140**

Digimon Level: **Ultimate**

Digimon Group: **Vegetation**

Digimon Type: **Data**

Data Size (G): **16.0**

Technique: **Flower Cannon**

Second Technique: **None**

Special Ability: **Flying**

Description: **Lillymon may look too cute to be tough, but beware. When it's shot out of a cannon, even a flower packs some punch. Lillymon is just as likely to fly away from trouble as fight.**

DIGIVOLVE

"JOE" JYO HIDO

Joe's a great guy, but he's not known for his bravery. When we first came to the Digital World, he said, "At a time like this, I think we'd be far better off just to find a cave and hide." He worries about his allergies and hay fever, and I think he kind of misses his mom. But I have to give Joe some credit—sometimes his worrying pays off. We've learned to pay better attention to his advice, because he spots danger better than the rest of us. And that's pretty important when you're being attacked by monsters the size of skyscrapers.

Bukamon

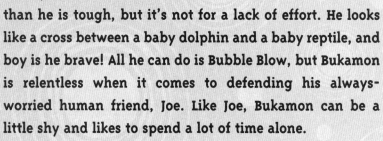

Pronunciation: **BOO-KAH-MON**

Number: **6**

Trading Card Number: **8**

Digimon Level: **In-Training**

Digimon Group: **Micro**

Data Size (G): **7.0**

Technique: **Bubble Blow**

Second Technique: **None**

Special Ability: **None**

IN-TRAINING

Description: **Bukamon is cuter than he is tough, but it's not for a lack of effort. He looks like a cross between a baby dolphin and a baby reptile, and boy is he brave! All he can do is Bubble Blow, but Bukamon is relentless when it comes to defending his always-worried human friend, Joe. Like Joe, Bukamon can be a little shy and likes to spend a lot of time alone.**

Bukamon digivolves into . . .

Gomamon

Pronunciation: **GOH-MAH-MON**

Number: **13**

Game Card Number: **St-11**

Trading Card Number: **15**

Digimon Level: **Rookie**

ROOKIE

Digimon Group: **Sea Animal**

Digimon Type: **Vaccine**

Data Size (G): **15.0**

Technique: **Marching Fishes**

Second Technique: **Claw Attack**

Special Ability: **Swimming**

Description: **Gomamon is a swimming fool! When he's on land, Gomamon is always antsy for the next chance to dive in and play in the water. In fact, he spends so much time in the water that he's befriended most of the fishes. That's how he saved all his Digimon and human friends from drowning—by carrying them off on a raft of Marching Fishes! He is also known for his curiosity.**

Gomamon digivolves into . . .

Ikkakumon

Pronunciation: **IH-KAH-KOO-MON**

Number: **28**

Game Card Number: **St–12**

Trading Card Number: **22**

Digimon Level: **Champion**

Digimon Group: **Sea Animal**

Digimon Type: **Vaccine**

Data Size (G): **25.0**

Technique: **Harpoon Torpedo**

Second Technique: **Heat Top**

Special Ability: **Swimming**

CHAMPION

Description: **Ikkakumon** looks like a combination of a walrus and a unicorn . . . only bigger! He is intensely loyal to Joe, and is one of the crew's toughest and most reliable Digimons. When Joe was attacked by Unimon in the deep snow, Gomamon digivolved into Ikkakumon, who knocked the Black Gear free from Unimon with his Harpoon Torpedo. Also, because Ikkakumon defeated the fierce Drimogemon at the submarine cave, the kids all earned Crest tags. He is specially adapted to icy surroundings—Ikkakumon can even melt ice so that he doesn't slip and fall.

Ikkakumon digivolves into . . .

Zudomon

Pronunciation: **ZOO-DOH-MON**

Number: **82**

Game Card Number: **St-38/69**

Digimon Level: **Ultimate**

Digimon Group: **Sea Animal**

Digimon Type: **Vaccine**

Data Size (G): **35.0**

Technique: **Vulcan's Hammer**

Second Technique: **Horn and Tusk**

Special Ability: **Swimming**

Description: **One look at a beast like Zudomon would send most humans and Digimons running for safety. His pointy spine, walrus tusks, vicious claws, and the giant Vulcan's Hammer he carries make him one of the most feared Digimons in DigiWorld.**

"T.K." TAKERU TAKAISHI

I can describe T.K. in one word: small. But he's only eight years old, so I guess that's natural. And to be fair, he's a lot braver than I was at that age. I mean, he does spend a lot of time trying to impress his big brother, Matt, who he really looks up to. But everyone likes T.K. because he's such a nice kid. Not to mention, when we're being attacked by scary Digimons like Seadramon, he stays pretty calm and relaxed. How can you not like a kid like that?

Tokomon

Pronunciation: **TOH-KOH-MON**
Number: **7**
Trading Card Number: **10**
Digimon Level: **In-Training**
Digimon Group: **Micro**
Data Size (G): **10.0**
Technique: **Bubble Blow**
Second Technique: **None**
Special Ability: **None**

Description: **Tokomon looks like a** cute little piglet. But don't sell him short. Even though he's pretty innocent, he doesn't have those fangs for nothing. He's as tough for his size as T.K., and won't back down from anyone. Still, Tokomon's main power is his enthusiasm under even the worst circumstances.

Tokomon digivolves into . . .

Patamon

Pronunciation: **PAT-AH-MON**

Number: **14**

Game Card Number: **St-13**

Trading Card Number: **17**

Digimon Level: **Rookie**

Digimon Group: **Mammal**

Digimon Type: **Data**

Data Size (G): **20.0**

Technique: **Boom Bubble**

Second Technique: **Slamming Attack**

Special Ability: **Flying**

Description: **Patamon might look like a mouse with wings, but when his Boom Bubble bursts in an opponent's face, it is fierce! Patamon is known for his obedience, and he defends T.K. with all his might. And when all else fails, he can even fly away really fast.**

ROOKIE

Patamon digivolves into . . .

Angemon

Pronunciation: **AN-JEE-MON**

Number: **43**

Game Card Number: **St-14**

Trading Card Number: **24**

Digimon Level: **Champion**

Digimon Group: **Angel**

Digimon Type: **Vaccine**

Data Size (G): **20.0**

Technique: **Hand of Fate**

Second Technique: **Angel Rod**

Special Ability: **Flying**

Description: **Angemon** could be called the Grand Angel of the DigiWorld. He is the exact opposite of Devimon, the devilish Digimon that has tainted the DigiWorld with pure evil in the form of Black Gears. When Angemon strikes Devimon with the powerful Hand of Fate, Devimon's evil ways are as good as destroyed. He is pure goodness, which in the DigiWorld always defeats evil.

CHAMPION

Angemon digivolves into . . .

MagnaAngemon

Pronunciation: **MAG-NAH-AN-GEE-MON**

Number: **88**

Game Card Number: **B0-142**

Digimon Level: **Ultimate**

Digimon Group: **Angel**

Digimon Type: **Vaccine**

Data Size (G): **24.0**

Technique: **The Gate of Destiny**

Second Technique: **Angel Rod**

Special Ability: **None**

Description: **If you think Angemon's Hand of Fate is an effective attack, wait until you see the Gate of Destiny. MagnaAngemon is Digiworld's version of a Super Angel, with the awesome ability to control an opponent's future.**

HARI

Kari is my one and only little sister, and, boy, was I happy to find her again when I got back to Earth through a crack in the DigiWorld. She's pretty smart, for a kid. For a while, though, she was definitely on the Evil Digimons' Most Wanted list. Everyone from king of the creeps Devimon to the bumbling Gotsumon wanted to capture her. Luckily she had her Digimon Gatomon on her side.

Salamon

Pronunciation: **SAL-AH-MON**

Digimon Level: **Rookie**

Digimon Group: **Unknown**

Digimon Type: **Unknown**

Data Size (G): **Unknown**

Special Ability: **None**

Description: **Very little is known about this Digimon, except that she is the Rookie form of Gatomon. Gatomon said that when she was Salamon, she was a slave to the evil Myotismon. He was very, very mean to her and scared her because he disliked her eyes. Gatomon remembers little else about when she was Salamon.**

ROOKIE

Salamon digivolves into . . .

Gatomon

Pronunciation: **GOT-OH-MON**

Number: **67**

Game Card Number: **Bo-15**

Digimon Level: **Champion**

Digimon Group: **Animal**

Digimon Type: **Vaccine**

Data Size (G): **10.0**

Technique: **Lightning Claw**

Second Technique: **Cat's Eye Hypnotism**

Special Ability: **None**

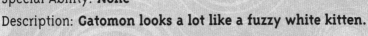

CHAMPION

Description: **Gatomon looks a lot like a fuzzy white kitten. That is, except for the enormous green and red claws and the tail that's two times as tall as her body. But if you're tempted to pet Gatomon, watch it. She's a Champion Digimon with one of the quickest attacks in DigiWorld—the Lightning Claw. After seeing Gatomon, you'll never look at your pet cat the same again.**

Gatomon digivolves into . . .

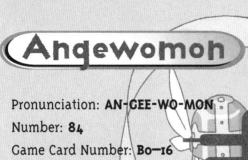

Angewomon

Pronunciation: **AN-GEE-WO-MON**

Number: **84**

Game Card Number: **Bo—16**

Digimon Level: **Ultimate**

Digimon Group: **Angel**

Digimon Type: **Vaccine**

Data Size (G): **20.0**

Technique: **Celestial Arrow**

Second Technique: **Hand of Fate**

Special Ability: **Flying**

Description: **Hey! Who's that woman (er, womon)? She looks fierce! That's Angewomon, the flying, heavenly angel monster of DigiWorld. She's tall and angelic, as her name suggests. You'll definitely be hypnotized by her Celestial Arrow and you won't want to be dealt her Hand of Fate.**

Kuwagamon

Pronunciation: **KOO-WAH-GAH-MON**
Number: **15**
Game Card Number: **Bo—13**
Trading Card Number: **25**
Digimon Level: **Champion**
Digimon Group: **Insectoid**
Digimon Type: **Virus**
Data Size (G): **20.0**
Technique: **Scissor Claw**
Second Technique: **Power Guillotine**
Special Ability: **Flying**

CHAMPION

Description: **Tai called him a "giant red beetle," but that doesn't quite capture it. Kuwagamon is a screeching red flying demon with enormous claws, gnashing pinchers, and an almost unstoppable attack technique: the Scissor Claw. He had no trouble defeating Agumon and almost caught Tai in the process.**

Shellmon

Pronunciation: **SHELL-MON**

Number: **17**

Game Card Number: **B0—09**

Digimon Level: **Rookie**

Digimon Group: **Sea Animal**

Digimon Type: **Data**

Data Size (G): **30.0**

Technique: **Hydro Blaster**

Second Technique: **Slamming Attack**

Special Ability: **Swimming**

ROOKIE

Description: **Shellmon is extremely tough for a rookie Digimon. He's an enormous pink sea monster with a spiny shell and a Medusa-like haircut. He surprise-attacked the kids from the ocean, shooting blasts of water at them with his Hydro Blaster attack technique. For Shellmon's second attack he slams opponents with his mammoth tail.**

Seadramon

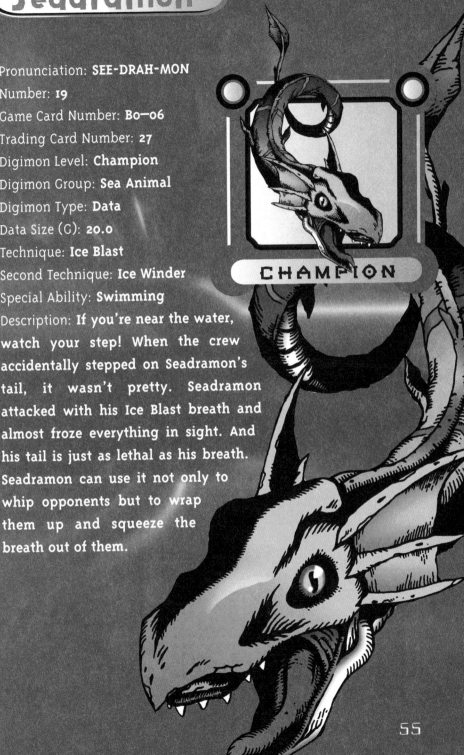

Pronunciation: **SEE-DRAH-MON**

Number: **19**

Game Card Number: **B0—06**

Trading Card Number: **27**

Digimon Level: **Champion**

Digimon Group: **Sea Animal**

Digimon Type: **Data**

Data Size (G): **20.0**

Technique: **Ice Blast**

Second Technique: **Ice Winder**

Special Ability: **Swimming**

Description: **If you're near the water, watch your step! When the crew accidentally stepped on Seadramon's tail, it wasn't pretty. Seadramon attacked with his Ice Blast breath and almost froze everything in sight. And his tail is just as lethal as his breath. Seadramon can use it not only to whip opponents but to wrap them up and squeeze the breath out of them.**

CHAMPION

Monochromon

Pronunciation: **MO-NOH-KROH-MON**

Number: **20**

Game Card Number: **B0—12**

Trading Card Number: **26**

Digimon Level: **Champion**

Digimon Group: **Dinosaur**

Digimon Type: **Data**

Data Size (G): **30.0**

Technique: **Volcanic Strike**

Second Technique: **Slamming Attack**

Special Ability: **None**

CHAMPION

Description: **Monochromon** may be a Dinosaur Digimon that looks like it's made of pure stone, but it is actually mellow. When the crew first runs into Monochromon, he is fighting another Monochromon for territory. It is not until later that the crew discovers the Monochromons are servants of Etemon, who controls the Server continent. The evil Etemon uses Monochromon to pull his heavy trailer.

Meramon

Pronunciation: **MEE-RAH-MON**

Number: **22**

Game Card Number: **B0—05**

Trading Card Number: **28**

Digimon Level: **Champion**

Digimon Group: **Fire**

Digimon Type: **Data**

Data Size (G): **18.0**

Technique: **Fireball**

Second Technique: **Burning Flame**

Special Ability: **None**

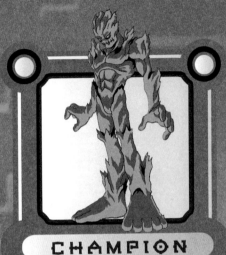

CHAMPION

Description: **Meramon** is a living, breathing being of flames who launches fireballs from his hands. He is the guardian of Mount Hiyarashi, and has been up to no good because of the Black Gear inside him. In fact, he even stopped the flow of the river so that it dried up completely. Luckily, before thousands of Digimons died of thirst, the kids and their Digimons fought Meramon and released his Black Gear.

Andromon

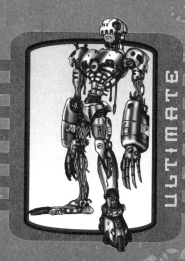

Pronunciation: **AN-DROH-MON**

Number: **24**

Game Card Number: **Bo-11**

Trading Card Number: **29**

Digimon Level: **Ultimate**

Digimon Group: **Android**

Digimon Type: **Vaccine**

Data Size (G): **25.0**

Technique: **Lightning Blade**

Second Technique: **Gatling Attack**

Special Ability: **None**

Description: **Andromon**'s not the kind of Digimon you want to mess with, especially if he's possessed by the Black Gear. He is an enormous Android Digimon with glowing blue eyes and metal arms that almost scrape the ground. When Andromon says, "Lightning Blade . . . fire!" during battle, everybody (digital or human) runs for cover. His eye sockets have an automatic radar screen that locates his opponents. Once his target is locked, Andromon's chest plates flip down and reveal missile launchers.

ULTIMATE

Numemon

Pronunciation: **NOO-MEE-MON**

Number: **26**

Game Card Number: **Bo–63**

Digimon Level: **Champion**

Digimon Group: **Mollusk**

Digimon Type: **Virus**

Data Size (G): **10.0**

Technique: **Party Time**

Second Technique: **Smash**

Special Ability: **Digging**

CHAMPION

Description: **Mimi described these** creatures just right when she said they were "like totally hygiene-deficient!! . . . And they had bad breath, too." For monsters that live in the sewer and look like insane balls of slime, though, Numemons aren't so bad. One of them even developed a crush on Mimi (can you blame him?) and saved her from Monzaemon's attack when he was infected with a Black Gear.

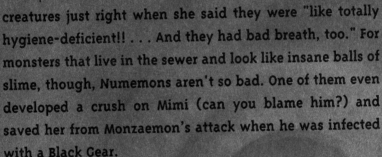

Unimon

Pronunciation: **YOO-NEE-MON**

Number: **29**

Game Card Number: **St—16/74**

Digimon Level: **Champion**

Digimon Group: **Mythical Animal**

Digimon Type: **Vaccine**

Data Size (G): **30.0**

Technique: **Aerial Attack**

Second Technique: **Sacred Blast**

Special Ability: **Flying**

Description: **If you like unicorns,**

CHAMPION

you'll love Unimon. He has the white-haired beauty and the one pointed horn of a unicorn. But he's also a Champion Digimon with a killer Aerial Attack! As the only known member of the Mythical Animal Digimon group, Unimon prowls the skies like a living airplane . . . with a lot of ammunition.

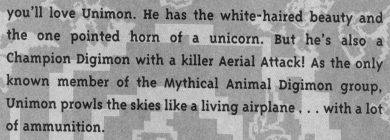

Leomon

Pronunciation: **LEE-OH-MON**

Number: **30**

Game Card Number: **B0—03**

Trading Card Number: **32**

Digimon Level: **Champion**

Digimon Group: **Animal**

Digimon Type: **Vaccine**

Data Size (G): **20.0**

Technique: **Fist of the Beast King**

Second Technique: **Beast Sword**

Special Ability: **None**

CHAMPION

Description: **Along with Angemon, Leomon is one of the most powerful of the *good* Digimons. But you wouldn't have guessed that at first. When the kids first met Leomon, he was a ferocious monster who threatened them with the Fist of the Beast King. But as soon as Tai used his digivice to release the Black Gear from Leomon's body, they realized how good-hearted he is. In no time, Leomon helped them cross the ocean to get to the continent of Server.**

Ogremon

Pronunciation: **OH-GURR-MON**
Number: **31**
Game Card Number: **Bo—04**
Trading Card Number: **33**
Digimon Level: **Champion**
Digimon Group: **Evil**
Digimon Type: **Virus**
Data Size (G): **20.0**
Technique: **Pummel Whack**
Second Technique: **Bone Cudgel**
Special Ability: **None**

CHAMPIO

Description: **Bright green skin. Teeth the size of your hands. Spikes coming out of his shoulders. Skull-and-crossbones tattoo on his arm. And in his hand, a huge club made out of bone. Could Ogremon be any more evil? Well, he's as evil as he looks. If Devimon is the King of Evil in DigiWorld, Ogremon is his ugly prince. The goodly Leomon found out just how evil he is when Ogremon attacked him with a vicious Pummel Whack of his bone club.**

Devimon

Pronunciation: **DEH-VEE-MON**
Number: **32**
Game Card Number: **B0—02**
Trading Card Number: **42**
Digimon Level: **Champion**
Digimon Group: **Evil**
Digimon Type: **Virus**
Data Size (G): **15.0**
Technique: **Touch of Evil**
Second Technique: **Evil Wing**
Special Ability: **Flying**
Description: **There is only**

CHAMPION

one word for Devimon: EVIL! He is the Dark Lord of Death, the Devil Monster, the enemy of every good Digimon. His evil plan is to take over File Island and then take over the world! His tactic: Devimon brainwashes good Digimons toward his evil ways by planting Black Gears in their bodies and then controlling their actions. His attack technique, the Touch of Evil, is one of the most feared attacks in DigiWorld.

Frigimon

CHAMPION

Pronunciation: **FRIH-GEE-MON**

Number: **33**

Game Card Number: **Bo—07**

Trading Card Number: **31**

Digimon Level: **Champion**

Digimon Group: **Icy**

Digimon Type: **Vaccine**

Data Size (G): **30.0**

Technique: **Subzero Ice Punch**

Second Technique: **Snow Ball**

Special Ability: **None**

Description: **Frigimon may look like a harmless, overgrown snowman, but when he attacks the kids with enormous snowballs and his infamous Subzero Ice Punch, he doesn't seem so harmless. The crew frees him from the evil influence of the Black Gear and wins Frigimon over to the good team! He stays with the kids and helps them defeat the evil Mojyamon.**

Mojyamon

Pronunciation: **MOH-JEE-AH-MON**

Number: **34**

Game Card Number: **Bo—14**

Digimon Level: **Champion**

Digimon Group: **Rare Animal**

Digimon Type: **Virus**

Data Size (G): **20.0**

Technique: **Ice Cloud**

Second Technique: **Bone Boomerang**

Special Ability: **None**

CHAMPION

Description: **If Bigfoot lived at the North Pole, it might look like Mojyamon. He's a huge, white furry beast with colossal paws. And if the kids hadn't become friends with Frigimon, Mojyamon would have frozen all of them with his Ice Cloud attack technique.**

Sukamon

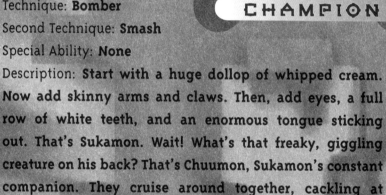

CHAMPION

Pronunciation: **SOO-KAH-MON**

Number: **35**

Game Card Number: **Bo—59**

Digimon Level: **Champion**

Digimon Group: **Mutant**

Digimon Type: **Virus**

Data Size (G): **10.0**

Technique: **Bomber**

Second Technique: **Smash**

Special Ability: **None**

Description: **Start with a huge dollop of whipped cream. Now add skinny arms and claws. Then, add eyes, a full row of white teeth, and an enormous tongue sticking out. That's Sukamon. Wait! What's that freaky, giggling creature on his back? That's Chuumon, Sukamon's constant companion. They cruise around together, cackling at themselves and bombing enemies for fun!**

Centarumon

Pronunciation: **SEN-TAR-OO-MON**

Number: **36**

Game Card Number: **St—17**

Digimon Level: **Champion**

Digimon Group: **Animal**

Digimon Type: **Data**

Data Size (G): **20.0**

Technique: **Solar Ray**

Second Technique: **Jet Gallop**

Special Ability: **None**

Description: **Yoinks! Sorry about that. It's just that Centarumon is** one of the scariest-looking Digimons in DigiWorld. And he *was* really scary when Mimi and Tentomon first met him in some ruins smack in the middle of a tropical rain forest. Luckily, it was just another case of Black Gear possession. Izzy got the Black Gear loose, and Centarumon showed he was actually one of the good Digimons when he defended the kids from Leomon's fierce attack.

CHAMPION

Bakemon

Pronunciation: **BAY-KEE-MON**

Number: **37**

Game Card Number: **St—45**

Trading Card Number: **34**

Digimon Level: **Champion**

Digimon Group: **Ghost**

Digimon Type: **Virus**

Data Size (G): **30.0**

Technique: **Dark Claw**

Second Technique: **Evil Charm**

Special Ability: **None**

CHAMPION

Description: **Bakemon is a Ghost Digimon, and not a very nice one at that. When he sees the kids roaming through his cemetery, Bakemon attacks them from the sky with his long Dark Claw. And a couple of Bakemons would have eaten Sora and Joe for dinner, if Joe hadn't foiled their plan by reciting special verses.**

Elecmon

Pronunciation: **EE-LEK-MON**

Number: **38**

Game Card Number: **B0—61**

Digimon Level: **Rookie**

Digimon Group: **Mammal**

Digimon Type: **Data**

Data Size (G): **20.0**

Technique: **Super Thunder Strike**

Second Technique: **Body Attack**

Special Ability: **Digging**

ROOKIE

Description: **If a red lizard sprouted tail feathers, it would look like Elecmon. But he's neither a bird nor a lizard. Elecmon is actually a Mammal Digimon, and he's deceptively tough for a rookie. Just when you think he'll get stepped on, Elecmon jolts his enemy with a vicious Super Thunder Strike! And if that doesn't work, he can always burrow into the earth and hide. His fierce side comes in handy when he's doing what he does best—caring for baby Digimons, and that includes protecting them from danger.**

Botamon

BABY

Pronunciation: **BOH-TAH-MON**

Number: **39**

Digimon Level: **Baby**

Digimon Group: **Micro**

Data Size (G): **5.0**

Technique: **Bubble Blow**

Second Technique: **None**

Special Ability: **None**

Description: **Botamon looks** like a bear cub . . . minus a body, that is. With a black fuzzy face and glowing yellow eyes, Botamon ranks up among the cutest Digimons. Unfortunately, he doesn't rank very high in the battle department.

Punimon

BABY

Pronunciation: **POO-NEE-MON**

Number: **40**

Digimon Level: **Baby**

Digimon Group: **Micro**

Data Size (G): **5.0**

Technique: **Bubble Blow**

Second Technique: **None**

Special Ability: **None**

Description: **Punimon might look like a drain plug, but don't sell him short. He's a great companion! This pink Micro Digimon might not win a battle against, say, Evilmon, but he won't back down either.**

Poyomon

Pronunciation: **POH-YOH-MON**

Number: **41**

Digimon Level: **Baby**

Digimon Group: **Micro**

Data Size (G): **5.0**

Technique: **Bubble Blow**

Second Technique: **None**

Special Ability: **None**

Description: **Boo! Is that a ghost? Or is that a kid trick-or-treating? Neither. That's Poyomon, the friendly ghost! He** just hovers around, completely see-through, with that goofy grin spread across his face, looking for DigiAction!

Yuramon

Pronunciation: **YER-AH-MON**

Number: **42**

Digimon Level: **Baby**

Digimon Group: **Micro**

Data Size (G): **5.0**

Technique: **Bubble Blow**

Second Technique: **None**

Special Ability: **None**

Description: **A floating fluff-**

ball with beady eyes, Yuramon is not exactly a warrior Digimon. A better description: Micro Digimon. With a Data Size of only 5.0 G, Yuramon's one of the smallest Digimons. But Yuramon is fast as lightning, and brave, too!

Whamon

Pronunciation: **WAH-MON**
Number: **44**
Game Card Number: **Bo—58**
Digimon Level: **Champion**
Digimon Group: **Sea Animal**
Digimon Type: **Vaccine**
Data Size (G): **40.0**
Technique: **Blasting Spout**
Second Technique: **Tidal Wave**
Special Ability: **Swimming**
Description: **Whale Monster.**

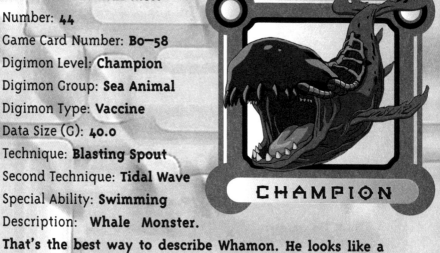

CHAMPION

That's the best way to describe Whamon. He looks like a whale, swims like a whale, he even has a Blasting Spout like a whale. So he must be a whale. But Whamon has more teeth than most whales, and he's actually nicer. The kids didn't think he was very nice when Whamon swallowed them whole. But when they removed the Black Gear from Whamon's stomach, he was so grateful that he transported them all to the continent of Server across the Ocean.

Drimogemon

Pronunciation: **DRIH-MOH-JEE-MON**

Number: **45**

Game Card Number: **Bo—10**

Digimon Level: **Champion**

Digimon Group: **Animal**

Digimon Type: **Data**

Data Size (G): **40.0**

Technique: **Iron Drill Spin, Crusher Bone**

Second Technique: **Mole's Claw**

Special Ability: **Digging**

Description: **Drimogemon might**

CHAMPION

look like a polar bear . . . if it weren't for the giant drill on his face! Even though Drimogemon doesn't look so nice, he's actually a good Digimon. He attacked the kids at a crucial point, while they searched for their "tags" underwater. But the kids' Digimons all digivolved and removed Drimogemon's Black Gear, and they've been buds with him ever since.

Etemon

Pronunciation: **EE-TEE-MON**

Number: **46**

Game Card Number: **B0—57**

Trading Card Number: **U3**

Digimon Level: **Ultimate**

Digimon Group: **Puppet**

Digimon Type: **Virus**

Data Size (G): **20.0**

Technique: **Dark Network, Concert Crush**

Second Technique: **Monkey Claw**

Special Ability: **None**

Description: **Etemon is a rock-and-roll monster! He wears shades. He carries a microphone around with him. He even travels in his own digital monster-mobile. Actually, the microphone is for communication only. (Fortunately for us, Etemon doesn't sing!) But don't underestimate Etemon. His Dark Network attack is a web of lines that can shoot down bolts and destroy anything within the net. Also, his Concert Crush attack can keep other Digimons from evolving into different forms.**

Gazimon

ROOKIE

Pronunciation: **GA-ZEE-MON**

Number: **47**

Game Card Number: **Bo—60**

Digimon Level: **Rookie**

Digimon Group: **Mammal**

Digimon Type: **Virus**

Data Size (G): **15.0**

Technique: **Electric Stun Blast**

Second Technique: **Pitfall**

Special Ability: **Digging**

Description: **The Gazimon might look** like cute little snow bunnies. But watch out! Because the Gazimon are not what they appear to be. They travel in packs and pick on others, and when they outnumber you they waste no time in sniping with their Electric Stun Blast. Ouch!

Paqumon

Pronunciation: **PAH-GOO-MON**
Number: **48**
Digimon Level: **Baby**
Digimon Group: **Micro**
Digimon Type: **Virus**
Data Size (G): **8.0**
Technique: **Bubble Blow**
Second Technique: **None**
Special Ability: **None**
Description: **Ya gotta admit it—the Pagumon, smiling little** puffballs who like to sing and dance, are kind of cute. But don't trust them, because they are really the tricksters of the DigiWorld. Once they even took over the Koromon's village and pretended it was theirs. Wow, the nerve!

BABY

SkullGreymon

Pronunciation: **SKULL-GRAY-MON**

Number: **49**

Game Card Number: **St—32**

Trading Card Number: **U4**

Digimon Level: **Ultimate**

Digimon Group: **Skeleton**

Digimon Type: **Virus**

Data Size (G): **40.0**

Technique: **Dark Shot**

Second Technique: **Double Dark Shot**

Special Ability: **None**

Description: **SkullGreymon is the dark skeleton of destruction. He's an Ultimate Digimon with pinching jaws like a killer dinosaur's, and prickly bones jutting from his back. He first showed up to defend the kids from a ferocious evil Greymon, but the kids got more than they'd bargained for when SkullGreymon also attacked several good Digimons. Proceed with caution.**

Kokatorimon

Pronunciation: **KOH-KAH-TO-REE-MON**

Number: **50**

Game Card Number: **Bo—56**

Trading Card Number: **34**

Digimon Level: **Champion**

Digimon Group: **Bird**

Digimon Type: **Data**

Data Size (G): **20.0**

Technique: **Frozen Fire Shot**

Second Technique: **Feather Sword**

Special Ability: **None**

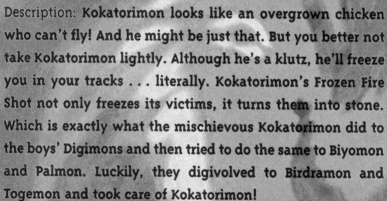

CHAMPION

Description: **Kokatorimon looks like an overgrown chicken who can't fly! And he might be just that. But you better not take Kokatorimon lightly. Although he's a klutz, he'll freeze you in your tracks . . . literally. Kokatorimon's Frozen Fire Shot not only freezes its victims, it turns them into stone. Which is exactly what the mischievous Kokatorimon did to the boys' Digimons and then tried to do the same to Biyomon and Palmon. Luckily, they digivolved to Birdramon and Togemon and took care of Kokatorimon!**

Tyrannomon

Pronunciation: **TIE-RAHN-OH-MON**

Number: **51**

Game Card Number: **Bo—66**

Digimon Level: **Champion**

Digimon Group: **Dinosaur**

Digimon Type: **Data**

Data Size (G): **20.0**

Technique: **Blaze Blast**

Second Technique: **Scratch**

Special Ability: **Digging**

Description: **Tyrannomon looks like the most ferocious dinosaur** that ever lived—the *Tyrannosaurus rex*. **And this Champion Digimon, who is one of Etemon's henchmen, is even more dangerous than the dinosaur it resembles. Because while** *T. rex* **only attacked with its powerful jaws and massive teeth, Tyrannomon strikes with his scorching Blaze Blast. Keep your distance.**

CHAMPION

Piximon

Pronunciation: **PIKS-EE-MON**
Number: **52**
Game Card Number: **St—30**
Trading Card Number: **U5**
Digimon Level: **Ultimate**
Digimon Group: **Pixie**
Digimon Type: **Data**
Data Size (G): **5.0**
Technique: **Pit Bomb**
Second Technique: **Fairy Tail**
Special Ability: **Flying**

Description: **Piximon is smaller than most In-Training Digimons. But sometimes mighty things come in small packages. Piximon is a famous Digimon trainer. Even though his methods are a bit wacky, they work, as the kids and their Digimon discover in a battle with Tyrannomon.**

Datamon

Pronunciation: **DAY-TAH-MON**

Number: **53**

Game Card Number: **Bo—67**

Digimon Level: **Ultimate**

Digimon Group: **Android**

Digimon Type: **Virus**

Data Size (G): **5.0**

Technique: **Digital Bomb**

Second Technique: **Data Crusher**

Special Ability: **None**

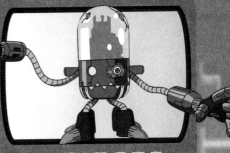

ULTIMATE

Description: **Datamon is another of the small-but-strong Ultimate Digimons. Datamon is like a bad disease. He's a Virus Digimon that invades the circuitry of other Digimons and causes them to malfunction. In a world where everything is made of digital material, that's a very powerful weapon to have. When the kids first met him, they freed him from Etemon. Then Datamon turned around and kidnapped Sora and Biyomon. Talk about ungrateful!**

Demidevimon

Pronunciation: **DEH-MEE-DEH-VEE-MON**

Number: **55**

Game Card Number: **St—42**

Digimon Level: **Champion**

Digimon Group: **Evil**

Digimon Type: **Virus**

Data Size (G): **8.0**

Technique: **Demi Dart**

Second Technique: **Evil Whisper**

Special Ability: **Flying**

Description: **Demidevimon**
is a mischievous little batlike
monster that pesters other Digimons while circling around
their heads. His Demi Dart attack surprises opponents with
its painful sting.

CHAMPION

Digitamamon

Pronunciation: **DI-JIT-AH-MAH-MON**

Number: **57**

Game Card Number: **Bo—70**

Digimon Level: **Ultimate**

Digimon Group: **Perfect**

Digimon Type: **Data**

Data Size (G): **10.0**

Technique: **Nightmare Syndrome**

Second Technique: **Hyper Flashing**

Special Ability: **None**

Description: **Don't look now . . . the egg has hatched! And whose crafty yellow eyes are those peering out from the eggshell? They're Digitamamon's. And you better keep your eyes open, because Digitamamon will cast a Nightmare Syndrome on you that'll make you wish you never went to sleep.**

Vegiemon

Pronunciation: **VEH-GEE-MON**

Number: **58**

Game Card Number: **Bo—135**

Digimon Level: **Champion**

Digimon Group: **Vegetation**

Digimon Type: **Virus**

Data Size (G): **10.0**

Technique: **Compost Bomber**

Second Technique: **Stink Jet**

Special Ability: **None**

Description: **This Vegiemon**

CHAMPION

doesn't look much like a veggie. If that thing shows up on your dinner plate, don't eat it. Because not only will the feathers on Vegiemon's head stick in your throat, but he might launch a Compost Bomber in your stomach!

Myotismon

Pronunciation: **MEE-OH-TIS-MON**

Number: **59**

Game Card Number: **Bo—38**

Digimon Level: **Ultimate**

Digimon Group: **Evil**

Digimon Type: **Virus**

Data Size (G): **18.0**

Technique: **Grisly Wing**

Second Technique:

Nightmare Claw

Special Ability: **None**

ULTIMATE

Description: **If the bats circling** around Myotismon's head didn't tip you off . . . he's evil. Other clues that Myotismon is among Devimon's crew of Evil Digimons are: the long black cape, the bony skeleton fingers, and the sinister grin on his face. Myotismon might be skinny, but when he opens his cape and unleashes the Grisly Wing attack, he won't seem so skinny anymore.

Vademon

Pronunciation: **VAY-DEE-MON**

Number: **60**

Game Card Number: **Bo—144**

Digimon Level: **Ultimate**

Digimon Group: **Alien**

Digimon Type: **Virus**

Data Size (G): **20.0**

Technique: **Unidentified Flying Kiss**

Second Technique: **Alien Ray**

Special Ability: **None**

Description: **If aliens look anything like Vademon, it's good that we haven't made contact with them. Because he's the ultimate in ugly. His see-through skull, purple brain, razor-thin body, and tubular legs form one of the strangest creatures in DigiWorld. And if that isn't weird enough, his attack technique is in the form of a kiss! Gross.**

Pabumon

Pronunciation: **PAH-BOO-MON**

Number: **61**

Digimon Level: **In-Training**

Digimon Group: **Micro**

Data Size (G): **5.0**

Technique: **Bubble Blow**

Second Technique: **None**

Special Ability: **None**

Description: **Pabumon is like a living soap bubble. And to be totally honest, he's about as intimidating—he even sucks on a pacifier! Not too fierce. At a size of 5.0 G and with a Bubble Blow technique, Pabumon's best bet is to run for cover!**

Gekomon

CHAMPION

Pronunciation: **GEH-KOH-MON**
Number: **62**
Game Card Number: **St—27**
Digimon Level: **Champion**
Digimon Group: **Amphibian**
Digimon Type: **Virus**
Data Size (G): **15.0**
Technique: **Symphony Crusher**
Second Technique: **Tongue Attack**
Special Ability: **None**
Description: **Gekomon looks like a lizard that drank too much gasoline. He seems harmless enough . . . until that hornlike thing blows you away with a loud Symphony Crusher. Or even worse, Gekomon could attack with that disgusting three-prong tongue. Watch out! These Digimons work for Shogunmon.**

Otamamon

Pronunciation: **OH-TAH-MAH-MON**

Number: **63**

Game Card Number: **St—24**

Digimon Level: **Rookie**

Digimon Group: **Amphibian**

Digimon Type: **Virus**

Data Size (G): **10.0**

Technique: **Stun Bubble**

Second Technique: **Slamming Attack**

Special Ability: **Swimming**

Description: **Otamamon looks like a purple blowfish with hands and a whip-tail. An excellent swimmer, Otamamon blows his infamous Stun Bubble through the water at opponents, rendering them totally useless. He's a Digimon with big plans—to revive Tonosama Gekomon.**

Shogunmon

Pronunciation: **SHOH-GUN-MON**

Number: **64**

Game Card Number: **Bo—08**

Digimon Level: **Champion**

Digimon Group: **Amphibian**

Digimon Type: **Virus**

Data Size (G): **20.0**

Technique: **Musical Fist**

Second Technique: **Frog Kick**

Special Ability: **None**

CHAMPION

Description: **He is the Gekomon's master, although he was asleep for three hundred years after he lost a singing contest. Talk about a sore loser! The only way to wake him up is to have someone with a beautiful voice sing for him. So the Gekomon kidnapped Mimi to sing for their master, and he woke up . . . but, boy, he was not a morning person.**

Flymon

Pronunciation: **FLY-MON**

Number: **66**

Game Card Number: **B0—128**

Digimon Level: **Champion**

Digimon Group: **Insectoid**

Digimon Type: **Virus**

Data Size (G): **20.0**

Technique: **Brown Stinger**

Second Technique: **Poison Powder**

Special Ability: **Flying**

CHAMPION

Description: **Imagine a fly that grew and grew until it was bigger than anyone you knew. Then add some huge pinchers, pink wings, and a Brown Stinger attack that knocks you into next week. What have you got? Flymon.**

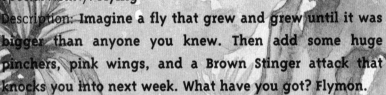

Nanimon

Pronunciation: **NA-NEE-MON**

Number: **68**

Game Card Number: **St—15**

Digimon Level: **Champion**

Digimon Group: **Invader**

Digimon Type: **Virus**

Data Size (G): **10.0**

Technique: **Power Punch**

Second Technique: **Puncher**

Special Ability: **None**

Description: **Look at the size**

CHAMPION

of those fists! The better to punch you with, my dear. Because that's all Nanimon does. Whether it's the Power Punch or the Puncher, Nanimon will keep swinging until his opponent hits the dirt.

Devidramon

Pronunciation: **DEH-VEE-DRAH-MON**

Number: **69**

Game Card Number: **Bo—132**

Digimon Level: **Champion**

Digimon Group: **Dragon**

Digimon Type: **Virus**

Data Size (G): **30.0**

Technique: **Crimson Claw**

Second Technique: **None**

Special Ability: **Flying**

Description: **Devil. Dragon. Wolf. Devidramon looks like a combination of all those things.** If that isn't intimidating enough, Devidramon lashes out at opponents with his terrifying Crimson Claw.

CHAMPION

Dokugumon

Pronunciation: **DOH-KOO-GOO-MON**

Number: **70**

Game Card Number: **St—19**

Digimon Level: **Champion**

Digimon Group: **Insectoid**

Digimon Type: **Virus**

Data Size (G): **30.0**

Technique: **Poison Thread**

Second Technique: **Poison Cobweb**

Special Ability: **None**

Description: **If a tick joined a motorcycle gang, it would**

CHAMPION

look like Dokugumon. He has a yellow helmet (or is that his head?) with two horns, a skull-and-crossbones on his back, and six legs. Beware! That skull-and-crossbones on Dokugumon's back is not just for decoration, it's a warning. Because both of Dokugumon's attack techniques are *extremely* poisonous.

Mammothmon

Pronunciation: **MAM-MOTH-MON**

Number: **71**

Game Card Number: **St-46**

Digimon Level: **Champion**

Digimon Group: **Ancient Animal**

Digimon Type: **Vaccine**

Data Size (G): **40.0**

Technique: **Tusk Crusher**

Second Technique: **Freezing Breath**

Special Ability: **None**

Description: **That's the strangest looking elephant in the world! Oh wait, no. That's Mammothmon, with a long snout, two huge tusks, wings, and a fuzzy body. He looks a lot like the now-extinct woolly mammoth that used to roam the earth. Mammothmon is a Champion Digimon, and he's tough as nails. If he doesn't crush his enemies with those pointy tusks, he'll freeze them with his breath. Luckily, he's a good Digimon.**

CHAMPION

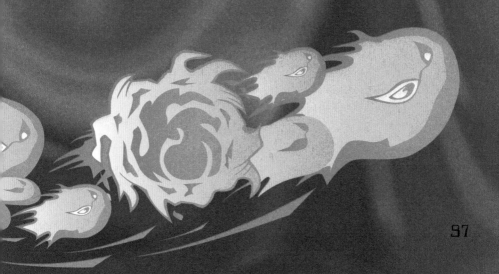

Gesomon

Pronunciation: **GEE-SOH-MON**

Number: **72**

Game Card Number: **B0—30**

Digimon Level: **Champion**

Digimon Group: **Sea Animal**

Digimon Type: **Virus**

Data Size (G): **30.0**

Technique: **Coral Crusher**

Second Technique: **Elastic Arms**

Special Ability: **Swimming**

CHAMPION

Description: **Gesomon looks like . . . okay, he doesn't look like anything. A big white shapeless beast with rubbery arms, gigantic teeth, and fins for a head, Gesomon is the terror of the seas. This Champion Sea Animal Digimon swims around searching for prey that he can attack with his Elastic Arms, or even worse, his powerful Coral Crusher technique. Hope you can swim fast!**

Raremon

Pronunciation: **RARE-EE-MON**
Number: **73**
Digimon Level: **Champion**
Digimon Group: **Evil**
Digimon Type: **Virus**
Data Size (G): **20.0**
Technique: **Breath of Decay**
Special Ability: **None**
Description: **There's no other way to say it: Raremon is just flat-out disgusting. If** you didn't gather as much by his slimy body and slobbering mouth, you should smell Raremon's breath! Whew! If Raremon unleashes the Breath of Decay on his victim, the stench will never be forgotten.

SkullMeramon

Pronunciation: **SKUL-MEH-RAH-MON**

Number: **74**

Game Card Number: **St—48**

Digimon Level: **Ultimate**

Digimon Group: **Fire**

Digimon Type: **Data**

Data Size (G): **20.0**

Technique: **Metal Fireball**

Second Technique: **Flame Chain**

Special Ability: **None**

Description: **SkullMeramon** looks like a flaming demon with a stitched-up mouth. His body is like a human's, but his form is definitely not. In place of skin, he has pure fire. And if that's not scary enough, wait until SkullMeramon hurls a Metal Fireball in your direction.

ULTIMATE

Wizardmon

Pronunciation: **WIH-ZARD-MON**

Number: **75**

Game Card Number: **St—44**

Digimon Level: **Champion**

Digimon Group: **Wizard**

Digimon Type: **Data**

Data Size (G): **15.0**

Technique: **Thunder Ball**

Second Technique: **Magical Game**

Special Ability: **None**

CHAMPION

Description: **Wizardmon is just that—a wizard monster. Wizardmon used to be a bad guy and worked for Myotismon. But then he changed his ways completely. He befriended Gatomon and the humans. The Thunder Ball that he unleashes from his fingertips packs the power of real thunder, and his Magical Game is lethal. Surprisingly, though, he is a bit shy.**

Pumpkinmon

Pronunciation: **PUMP-KIN-MON**

Number: **76**

Game Card Number: **Bo-37**

Digimon Level: **Ultimate**

Digimon Group: **Puppet**

Digimon Type: **Data**

Data Size (G): **20.0**

Technique: **Trick or Treat**

Second Technique:

Pumpkin Squash

Special Ability: **None**

Description: **Trick or Treat? With Pumpkinmon, you better choose neither. Because Pumpkinmon, a walking pumpkin with an axe sticking out of his head, is the Halloween Monster of DigiWorld. And "Trick or Treat" is not a playful question, it's Pumpkinmon's attack technique! Although he is a bad Digimon, most of the time he just wants to have fun.**

Gotsumon

Pronunciation: **GOT-SOO-MON**

Number: **77**

Game Card Number: **St—23**

Digimon Level: **Rookie**

Digimon Group: **Rock**

Digimon Type: **Data**

Data Size (G): **20.0**

Technique: **Rock Fist**

Second Technique: **Crazy Crusher**

Special Ability: **Digging**

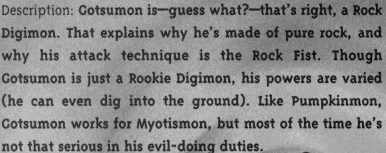

Description: **Gotsumon is—guess what?—that's right, a Rock Digimon. That explains why he's made of pure rock, and why his attack technique is the Rock Fist. Though Gotsumon is just a Rookie Digimon, his powers are varied (he can even dig into the ground). Like Pumpkinmon, Gotsumon works for Myotismon, but most of the time he's not that serious in his evil-doing duties.**

103

Phantomon

Pronunciation: **FAN-TOH-MON**

Number: **79**

Game Card Number:

Bo—39

Digimon Level: **Ultimate**

Digimon Group: **Ghost**

Digimon Type: **Virus**

Data Size (G): **15.0**

Technique: **Shadow Scythe**

Second Technique: **Father Time**

Special Ability: **None**

Description: **Who is that hiding beneath the hood? It's Phantomon, who attacks at will with the golden Shadow Scythe that he carries around. If the scythe doesn't slice the way he wants, Phantomon will strike with his more conceptual attack—Father Time. He also works for Myotismon.**

DarkTyrannomon

Pronunciation: **DARK-TIE-RAH-NO-MON**

Number: **80**

Game Card Number: **Bo—79**

Digimon Level: **Champion**

Digimon Group: **Dinosaur**

Digimon Type: **Virus**

Data Size (G): **40.0**

Technique: **Fire Blast**

Second Technique: **None**

Special Ability: **None**

CHAMPION

Description: **Run for your life! That's your best bet of** fending off DarkTyrannomon, the massive black Champion Dinosaur Digimon with razor-sharp teeth and a powerful Fire Blast attack. He's yet another of Myotismon's henchmen.

Gizamon

Pronunciation: **GIH-ZAH-MON**

Number: **81**

Game Card Number: **Bo—71**

Trading Card Number:

Digimon Level: **Rookie**

Digimon Group: **Mammal**

Digimon Type: **Data**

Data Size (G): **15.0**

Technique: **Spiral Saw**

Special Ability: **None**

Description: **Gizamon** looks a

little like a frog. Except, of course, for the four razor-sharp fins on his back. And the porcupine hair. Oh, yeah. There are also the extra-long claws. So actually, Gizamon doesn't look that much like a frog, especially when he tries to saw his opponents in half with the Spiral Saw attack.

MegaSeadramon

Pronunciation: **MEH-GA-SEE-DRAH-MON**

Number: **83**

Game Card Number: **B0—31**

Digimon Level: **Ultimate**

Digimon Group: **Sea Animal**

Digimon Type: **Data**

Data Size (G): **25.0**

Technique: **Thunder Javelin**

Second Technique: **Mega Ice Blast**

Special Ability: **Swimming**

Description: **MegaSeadramon might have been a sea horse at one point, before something went dreadfully wrong. Because now he is a coily sea serpent with scales, tusk, and several rows of teeth. MegaSeadramon is a skilled swimmer with a Thunder Javelin attack that is tough to defend against underwater.**

Tuskmon

Pronunciation: **TUSK-MON**
Number: **85**
Game Card Number: **Bo—75**
Digimon Level: **Champion**
Digimon Group: **Dinosaur**
Digimon Type: **Virus**
Data Size (G): **40.0**
Technique: **Slamming Tusk**
Second Technique: **Horn Buster**

CHAMPION

Description: **Watch out for that . . . tusk! Tuskmon not only has all the weapons of the other Dinosaur Digimons (including a whip-tail, a spiny back, and huge claws), he also has a pointy tusk on his snout that he slams into opponents with ferocity.**

Snimon

Pronunciation: **SNEE-MON**

Number: **86**

Game Card Number: **B0—25**

Digimon Level: **Champion**

Digimon Group: **Insectoid**

Digimon Type: **Vaccine**

Data Size (G): **30.0**

Technique: **Twin Sickles**

Second Technique:
Slamming Attack

Special Ability: **None**

CHAMPION

Description: **What is that big green . . . thing? That's Snimon. And it's not the green skin that you have to worry about, it's those two silver knifelike things that Snimon has for arms. They're called Twin Sickles, and they can slice opponents into fourths in no time.**

VenomMyotismon

Pronunciation: **VEH-NOM-MEE-YOH-TIS-MON**

Number: **89**

Game Card Number:

St—97

Digimon Level: **Mega**

Digimon Group: **Evil**

Digimon Type: **Virus**

Data Size (C): **38.0**

Technique: **Venom**

Infusion

Second Technique:

Nightmare Claw

Special Ability: **None**

Description: VenomMyotismon is up with Devimon in terms of pure evil. He is Myotismon's fully evolved superself, a towering, energy-devouring monster. He looks vampire-ish, much like Myotismon, but his Venom Infusion is one of the most deadly attacks in DigiWorld.

Chuumon

Pronunciation: **CHOO-MON**

Number: **92**

Game Card Number:

Digimon Level: **Champion**

Digimon Group: **Animal**

Digimon Type: **Virus**

Data Size (G): **Unknown**

Special Ability: **None**

Description: **Chuumon is Sukamon's right-hand man,**

CHAMPION

uh, monster, and what a pair they make. When Sukamon is not bombing other Digimons, he and Chuumon do nothing but giggle like a couple of two-year-olds. What a goofball! Chuumon and Sukamon live in a tropical rain forest and they share one brain between the two of them.

MetalSeadramon

Pronunciation: **MEH-TUL-SEE-DRAH-MON**
Number: **93**
Game Card Number: **Bo—35**
Digimon Level: **Mega**
Digimon Group: **Android**
Digimon Type: **Data**
Data Size (G): **30.0**
Technique: **River of Power**
Second Technique: **Giga Ice Blast**
Special Ability: **Swimming**
Description: **He is one of the Dark Masters, the most** evil of all the Digimons in the DigiWorld. He has been known to say, "I rule this ocean with an iron hand, and an iron tail, and an iron everything for that matter." Whoa! He means business.

Machinedramon

Pronunciation: **MAH-SHEEN-DRAH-MON**

Number: **95**

Game Card Number: **Bo—55**

Digimon Level: **Mega**

Digimon Group: **Machine**

Digimon Type: **Virus**

Data Size (G): **40.0**

Technique: **Giga Cannon**

Second Technique: **Dragon Fire**

Special Ability: **None**

Description: **Robot on the**
loose! Machinedramon is a Machine Digimon with a Giga Cannon that blows opponents away. He is one of the Four Dark Masters.

Piedmon

Pronunciation: **PIED-MON**

Number: **96**

Game Card Number: **B0—42**

Digimon Level: **Mega**

Digimon Group: **Evil**

Digimon Type: **Virus**

Data Size (G): **18.0**

Technique: **Trump Sword**

Second Technique: **Crown Trick**

Special Ability: **None**

Description: **Piedmon is one of the most powerful and magical of tricksters. Piedmon attacks with sorcery and sleight of hand. Even his weapon, the Trump Sword, catches opponents off guard. He is one of the four Dark Masters.**

Puppetmon

Pronunciation: **PUH-PET-MON**

Number: **97**

Game Card Number: **Bo—96**

Digimon Level: **Mega**

Digimon Group: **Puppet**

Digimon Type: **Virus**

Data Size (G): **10.0**

Technique: **Puppet Pummel**

Second Technique: **Wires**

Choking

Special Ability: **None**

Description: **If there were**

such a thing as an evil puppet, it would be Puppetmon.
He's one of the four Dark Masters, the most evil Digimons in
the DigiWorld. Yikes, you definitely want to be the one
pulling his strings and not the other way around.

Skorpiomon

Pronunciation: **SKOR-PEE-OH-MON**

Number: **98**

Game Card Number: **Bo—32**

Digimon Level: **Ultimate**

Digimon Group: **Crustacea**

Digimon Type: **Data**

Data Size (G): **20.0**

Technique: **Tail Blade**

Second Technique: **Twin Sword**

Special Ability: **Swimming**

Description: **Scorpiomon is a scorpion . . . squared! His Tail Blade is one of the most dangerous weapons in DigiWorld. One smack with the Tail Blade could end a battle with the toughest of Champion Digimons. And if that doesn't work, Scorpiomon uses the Twin Sword on his back to defend himself.**

Kiwimon

Pronunciation: **KEE-WEE-MON**

Number: **100**

Game Card Number: **Bo—85**

Digimon Level: **Champion**

Digimon Group: **Ancient Bird**

Digimon Type: **Data**

Data Size (G): **15.0**

Technique: **Pummel Peck**

Second Technique: **High Jumping Kick**

Special Ability: **None**

Description: **Whoa! Is that an overgrown ostrich? Nope. That's Kiwimon, the Champion Ancient Bird Digimon with a skull head, a vicious Pummel Peck attack, and a very bad attitude.**

CHAMPION

Mushroomon

Pronunciation: **MUSH-ROO-MON**

Number: **101**

Game Card Number: **Bo—82**

Digimon Level: **Rookie**

Digimon Group: **Vegetation**

Digimon Type: **Virus**

Data Size (G): **12.0**

Technique: **Fungus Cruncher**

Second Technique: **Laughing Smasher**

Special Ability: **None**

Description: **There's a fungus among us! Mushroomon, that is, the Rookie Digimon that looks like an overgrown, overly happy mushroom. But this monster is no ordinary pizza topping. Mushroomon's Fungus Cruncher packs quite a punch, and his Laughing Smasher will leave you in stitches.**

Floramon

Pronunciation: **FLOR-AH-MON**

Number: **103**

Game Card Number: **Bo-81**

Digimon Level: **Rookie**

Digimon Group: **Vegetation**

Digimon Type: **Data**

Data Size (G): **10.0**

Technique: **Rain of Pollen**

Second Technique: **Stamen Rope**

Special Ability: **None**

ROOKIE

Description: **Floramon is one weird creature. Just to throw everyone off the trail, he is a Vegetation Digimon but evolves like a reptile. Got that? Even his roommates at Pinokkion Mansion are confused by this one.**

MetalEtemon

Pronunciation: **MEH-TAL-EE-TEE-MON**

Game Card Number: **Bo—27**

Digimon Level: **Mega**

Digimon Group: **Android**

Digimon Type: **Virus**

Data Size (G): **30.0**

Technique: **Slippery Banana**

Second Technique: **Metal Punch**

Special Ability: **None**

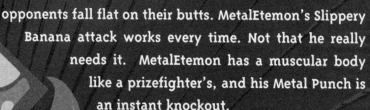

Description: *"What was thaaaaaattttttt?"* That's the last thing you hear before opponents fall flat on their butts. MetalEtemon's Slippery Banana attack works every time. Not that he really needs it. MetalEtemon has a muscular body like a prizefighter's, and his Metal Punch is an instant knockout.

Mekanorimon

Pronunciation: **MEH-KAN-OR-EE-MON**

Number: **106**

Game Card Number: **St—86**

Digimon Level: **Champion**

Digimon Group: **Machine**

Digimon Type: **Virus**

Data Size (G): **25.0**

Technique: **Twin Beam**

Second Technique: **None**

Special Ability: **None**

CHAMPION

Description: **Mekanorimon is a motorized fighting machine. His super-long, metal arms can** either pummel opponents or blow them away with the Twin Beam blaster.

RedVegiemon

Pronunciation: **RED-VEH-JEE-MON**

Number: **109**

Game Card Number: **Bo—87**

Digimon Level: **Champion**

Digimon Group: **Vegetation**

Digimon Type: **Virus**

Data Size (G): **12.0**

Technique: **Rotten Rainballs**

Second Technique: **Poison Ivy**

Special Ability: **Digging**

CHAMPION

Description: **RedVegiemon is kind of like a vine-ripened, stronger version of Vegiemon. But** he's hardly a harmless vegetable—he'll do anything that his boss, Puppetmon, tells him to do, and if that means using his Poison Ivy technique to make his enemies so itchy that they beg for mercy, he's up for the job anytime, anywhere.

Tankmon

Pronunciation: **TANK-MON**

Number: **III**

Digimon Level: **Champion**

Digimon Group: **Android**

Digimon Type: **Data**

Data Size (G): **35.0**

Technique: **Hyper Cannon**

Second Technique: **Machine Gun Arm**

Special Ability: **Digging**

Description: **This guy's a tank . . .**

CHAMPION

literally. Tankmon is a living, breathing army tank with sand-roving skills, Hyper Cannon attack, Machine Gun Arm, and a big smile on his tank face.

129

Hahgurumon

Pronunciation: **HAH-GOO-ROO-MON**

Number: **112**

Game Card Number: **St—64**

Digimon Level: **Rookie**

Digimon Group: **Machine**

Digimon Type: **Virus**

Data Size (G): **12.0**

Technique: **Darkness Gear**

Second Technique: **Drag**

Special Ability: **None**

Description: **Hahgurumon is a gear monster, and when he joins up with other gears, he's** pretty tough. But on a solo mission, Hahgurumon is just a Rookie Digimon with average powers.

ROOKIE

Warumonzaemon

Pronunciation: **WAH-ROO-MON-ZAY-MON**

Number: **113**

Game Card Number: **St—83**

Digimon Level: **Ultimate**

Digimon Group: **Puppet**

Digimon Type: **Virus**

Data Size (G): **24.0**

Technique: **Heart Break Attack**

Second Technique: **Bear Claw**

Special Ability: **None**

Description: **Attack of the killer teddy bear! With his vicious Heart Break Attack, Warumonzaemon is as scary as a kid's toy could possibly be.**

ULTIMATE

LadyDevimon

Pronunciation: **LAY-DEE-DEH-VEE-MON**

Game Card Number: **Bo—22**

Digimon Level: **Ultimate**

Digimon Group: **Evil**

Digimon Type: **Virus**

Data Size (G): **20.0**

Technique: **Darkness Poison**

Second Technique: **Black Wing**

Special Ability: **Flying**

Description: **Oooh! Scary! This spooky lady is a member of the Nightmare Soldiers. Her enemies would be wise to keep a flashlight handy if they think she's going to be around, because LadyDevimon is likely to show up at night.**

Pronunciation: **EE-VIL-MON**

Number: **115**

Game Card Number: **Bo—20**

Digimon Level: **Champion**

Digimon Group: **Evil**

Digimon Type: **Virus**

Technique: **Nightmare Shocker**

Second Technique: **Scratch**

Special Ability: **Flying**

Description: **Imagine a bat crossed with a werewolf,** crossed with a flying dinosaur, crossed with a mad demon. Give up? You will if you come across Evilmon. The name says it all. Evilmon is pure evil, and his Nightmare Shocker turns normal Digimons into raving lunatics.

CHAMPION

Monzaemon

Pronunciation: **MON-ZAY-MON**

Number: **27**

Game Card Number: **Bo—62**

Trading Card Number: **30**

Digimon Level: **Ultimate**

Digimon Group: **Puppet**

Digimon Type: **Vaccine**

Data Size (G): **40.0**

Technique: **Hearts Attack**

Second Technique: **Hug**

Special Ability: **None**

Description: **Monzaemon** is the leader of Toy Town, where toys that have been thrown away go to live. He looks like a huge, sweet teddy bear. When he's infected by a Black Gear, he turns evil and shoots heat rays with his eyes and attacks his victims with heart-shaped balloons.

Divermon

Pronunciation: **DIE-VER-MON**
Number: **168**
Game Card Number: **St—82**
Digimon Level: **Ultimate**
Digimon Group: **Sea Animal**
Digimon Type: **Data**
Data Size (G): **20.0**
Technique: **Striking Fish**
Second Technique: **Fishing Rod**
Special Ability: **Swimming**

Description: **If you think sharks are scary, wait until you see this scuba freak! Divermon has flippers, a full tank of oxygen on his back, and a harpoon gripped in his enormous claws. And if that weren't intimidating enough, he swims like a fish and is a little, well, crazy. He works for MetalSeadramon.**

Blossomon

Pronunciation: **BLO-SO-MON**

Number: **178**

Game Card Number: **B0—90**

Digimon Level: **Ultimate**

Digimon Group: **Vegetation**

Digimon Type: **Data**

Data Size (G): **20.0**

Technique: **Spiral Flower**

Second Technique: **Thorn Whips**

Description: **If you thought veggies were harmless, wait until you meet Blossomon. Because this blossoming, teeth-gnashing beast will eat you for dinner! His rose-petal head fools many Digimons just long enough for Blossomon to launch an effective Spiral Flower attack.**

Deramon

Pronunciation: **DEE-RAH-MON**

Number: **179**

Game Card Number: **Bo—91**

Digimon Level: **Ultimate**

Digimon Group: **Bird**

Digimon Type: **Data**

Data Size (G): **25.0**

Technique: **Royal Smasher**

Second Technique: **Beak Buster**

Special Ability: **None**

Description: **Deramon is the Queen Bird Digimon. Though the huge** green bush of a tail on her back makes Deramon look pudgy, don't sell her short! Her Royal Smasher is a destructive force to be reckoned with.

Cherrymon

Pronunciation: **CHEH-REE-MON**

Number: **180**

Game Card Number: **B0—92**

Digimon Level: **Ultimate**

Digimon Group: **Vegetation**

Digimon Type: **Data**

Data Size (G): **40.0**

Technique: **Pit Pelter**

Second Technique: **Illusion Mist**

Special Ability: **None**

Description: **Take on this monster, and you'll be barking up the wrong tree. Because Cherrymon is** the most evil Cherry Tree you'll ever see. And when Cherrymon pelts opponents with cherry pits, it's not a moment they'll soon forget.

Garbagemon

Pronunciation: **GAR-BAJ-MON**

Number: **181**

Game Card Number: **Bo—93**

Digimon Level: **Ultimate**

Digimon Group: **Mutant**

Digimon Type: **Virus**

Data Size (G): **15.0**

Technique: **Junk Chunker**

Second Technique: **Dirty Saucer**

Special Ability: **None**

Description: **King of the Trash!**

The Junk Jester! Waste Can Wizard! Call this Digimon whatever you want, but don't get too close to the can. Because Garbagemon smells awful! And even if you're out of nose-range, it doesn't mean you're safe. Garbagemon can throw chunks of junk for several blocks.

SaberLeomon

Pronunciation: **SAY-BER-LEE-OH-MON**

Number: **192**

Game Card Number: **St—34**

Digimon Level: **Mega**

Digimon Group: **Ancient Animal**

Digimon Type: **Data**

Data Size (G): **20.0**

Technique: **Howling Crusher**

Second Technique: **Twin Fang**

Special Ability: **None**

MEGA

Description: **If you're not scared of the fluorescent yellow fur, you'll definitely shrink away from the two enormous "saber" fangs. If they don't get you, the gigantic paws and** Howling Crusher attack most definitely will.

Where is Server, and why is it so important?
Server is a continent in the DigiWorld. The kids are asked by Gennai to go there to fight Evil Digimons.

Is it true that Digimons with human counterparts are the only ones that digivolve from level to level?
Yes. The only Digimons that digivolve are those that belong to the kids. Why? In order to understand why, you must know the "Legend of the DigiDestined." According to ancient legend, there would come a time when DigiWorld would be taken over by a strange dark force that will change good Digimons into bad ones. That time has come, and the dark force is spread by Devimon with his evil Black Gears.

The legend also predicts that a group of children, called the "DigiDestined," would appear from another world. When they arrived, they would come to possess superpowers that eventually save DigiWorld from destruction.
Who are the DigiDestined, and what is their superpower?

The DigiDestined are the kids—Sora, Matt, Tai, and the whole squad—and their superpower is the power of digivolution. Their Digimons could not digivolve into bigger, tougher Digimons and defeat the powers of evil if not for the power from the kids and their digivices.

Where is DigiWorld?

Very good question. Is DigiWorld a planet, like earth? Or is

it an entirely different dimension? Hmmm. Certain incidents, like when the gang finds telephone booths, abandoned school buses, and even a group of candy machines, suggest that DigiWorld could even be on planet earth! But many other things suggest that DigiWorld is in an entirely different dimension. For example, everything in the DigiWorld is digital (how weird!), it's all controlled by a force on the continent of Server, and of course, there are monsters running around everywhere.

Still, despite all that, the most honest answer to this question is not very satisfying—WE DON'T KNOW. But if that's a huge bummer for you, it shouldn't be. Keep looking for clues and forming your own theories. Maybe you'll figure it out on your own. And don't despair; you will find out. Just keep watching the show.

What are the "tags" and the "crests"?

Tags and crests help the kids' Digimons digivolve to the next level. The tags were secretly hidden by the ultimate in Evil Digimons, Devimon, but the kids were able to find them in, of all places, an underwater convenience store. Talk about one-stop shopping! The crests are scattered throughout the continent of Server, and each Digidestined kid has his or her own crest, which reflects his or her personality. Tai's crest is Courage, Matt's is Friendship, Joe's is Reliability, Sora's is Love, Mimi's is Sincerity, T.K.'s is Hope, and Izzy's is Knowledge.

DIGIMON CARD GAME

Check out the superfun Digimon card game, DIGI-BATTLE, in toy stores now. Compete with your friends as your favorite Digimons digivolve and battle in an exciting card game filled with full-color collector's cards. But you better get your DIGI-BATTLE fast, before they're all gone!

DIGIMON COLLECTOR CARDS

You can find all your favorite Digimons in colorful, glossy collector cards from Upper Deck!

Ready for Battle Rookies! 2 of 10

Digivolving Roo

The seven in-training digivolve to rookie Di protect the kids and evil champion Digimo battle!

DIGIMON

© Akiyoshi Hongo • Toei Animation. TM and © 1999 B
card/hologram combination is a trademark of The Upper
Company, LLC. © 2000 The Upper Deck Company, LLC.
Reserved. Printed in the U.S.A.

DIGIMON

Ready for battle! Rookies!! DP 400

Rookie Digimons

T.U. SHOW

Will Tai, Sora, Matt, and the gang help save the DigiWorld from the forces of evil? Will they ever get home again? Find out for yourself. Catch an exciting Digimon adventure every day after school on Fox Kids!

ALPHABETICAL INDEX

141

143